★ ★ ★ ★ ★ ★ ★

BUSH LIES IN STATE

MALACHY McCOURT

SENSEI PUBLICATIONS
New York

ISBN 0-9755746-0-4

Several of the essays that appear in this book were
previously published in *The West Side Spirit*. The
author and publisher of this book thank *The Spirit*
for permission to reprint those articles here.

Manufactured in the United States of America

Foe bulk sales please contact the publisher at
senseiny@rcn.com

Contents

Cast
of
Characters

Blinky Bin Bush (*aka "Blinkman"*)—Our current, soon-to-be-ex-President

Mullah Cheney Dick—Our nearly begone Vice President

Condisleaze Rice—National Security Advisor

The Texiban—Blinky's posse (*sometimes referred to as his cabinet and advisors*)

Colin Pow-less—Blinky's enabler

St. John Faschcroft—Blinky's hyper-religious Deformer of the Laws

Big Blinky bin Bush—Blinky's earthly father

Richard Perleswine—Blinky's former cold-blooded warrior, "The Prince of Darkness"

Bush Lies in State

WE ALL KNOW what addicts (or alcoholics) are, don't we? They are guys who stick needles in their arms, or drink out of bottles ensconced in brown paper bags, who doze off in public places and mess their trousers.

If that's your answer, you'll be graded "four" on a scale of one hundred. Ninety-six out of every one hundred drinkers afflicted with the disease of alcoholism are folks you wouldn't give a second glance in the course of everyday life, for they are women in classy outfits, men in suits and ties, or younger folks in casual dress, many of whom are college students. And here begins our argument: George Walker Bush avers that he stopped "heavy" drinking a long time ago; despite strong anecdotal evidence, he has never admitted to cocaine use.

Now, Bill Clinton admits he tried marijuana but never

inhaled; similarly, George W. Bush may have "tried" cocaine and never sniffed, although he is often observed to sniffle a lot these days, an indication that he either has a permanent cold or permanent damage to his nasal membranes.

All alcoholics have things in common: the disease of alcoholism itself, for which there is no cure, the selfish, self-centered, uncaring behavior, and the delight often taken in other people's suffering. The disease is all about losing and humiliation, and the sooner the addict acknowledges his sickness, the quicker the road to recovery. Ceasing to drink is not in itself "recovery," nor is proclaiming (as does George W. Bush, our future-former President) that Jesus Christ, Esq., is his personal savings and loan man, not to mention his Savior and favorite philosopher. (Never mind that Georgie don't imitate Jesus in thought, word, or deed.)

The three components of this disease are physical, emotional, and spiritual. It is often envisioned as a living beast whose aim is to destroy its home—your body. It will ravage your liver and your stomach, and get you smoking so it can then destroy the lungs. It will likewise wreck your kidneys, cloud your judgment, deaden all love, and make you either impotent or a rapist (or both), and will do all this whilst fostering rages and fantasies so that normal family life becomes impossible.

In attacking the spirit, it aims to separate a person from all that is wondrous and beautiful in the mind, the intellect, and the world—the sun, the moon, the mountains, and any merciful deity of any sort whatsoever. Most important, it discards the truth as if it were a disgusting lump of flesh in the last stages of putrefaction.

There are four kinds of alcoholic: (1) the active (still drinking) alcoholic; (2) the dry-drunk alky, (3) the recovering alcoholic, who is well on the way to regaining physical, emotional, and spiritual health, and (4) the fully recovered alcoholic (the only qualification for a full recovery from alcoholism is to be dead and buried, so we need not deal with No. 4).

Much more dangerous than the boozing alcoholic is the "dry drunk," a type clearly illustrated by our current near-future-former President. George W's abundant symptoms are typical of all Dry Drunks (DDs), who are angry because they are drunks, always wanting a drink, and they hate people like themselves, so they are continuously vengeful and judgmental, and they always, always are liars. Being both boastful and cowardly, they secretly proclaim their superiority to any other persons on earth, even whilst they pretend to be average, nose-to-the-grindstone jerks.

When George W. applied to the Texas Air National Guard, he stated that he would not volunteer for overseas duty, which led Senator (and war hero) John McCain to remark that he slept better at night when he was a P.O.W. in Vietnam, knowing that Bush was defending the coast of Texas. Brave boy, George!

In the eye-opening book on Bush's dismal military career, *Fortunate Son*, by J. H. Hatfield, one officer, Colonel Ralph Anderson, relates that many's the night George stripped off his uniform and danced naked on a bar whilst lip-synching to George Jones' song, "White Lightning." No doubt he would have been decorated for that heroic act had he been wearing his uniform. Hatfield also remarked that Fortunate Bush screwed more girls than Hugh Hefner.

A mere 600-plus Americans have been killed since May 2, 2003, when George W., "misunderestimating" our victory, landed on the aircraft carrier U.S.S. Lincoln, decked out in full flight gear. This was a truly dangerous task, since the ship was 100 miles off the coast of California, which still had a Democratic governor. During the Vietnam War, however, someone had to stay home and take care of the nasty business of making money; many of those who managed to dodge that war later became cheerleaders for others to go off and fight, including George W. Bush, Danny "Potatoe" Quayle, the Cheney Dick, his assistant Lewis "Scooter" Libby, White House Chief-of-Staff Andy Card, Deputy Secretary of Defense Paul Wolfowitz, "The Prince of Darkness," Richard Perle, former Press Secretary Ari Fleischer, N.S.C. Director Elliot Abrahms, White House Adviser Karl ("Dirty Tricks") Rove, Jesus Christ's representative-on-Earth, John Ashcroft, DEA Director, Asa Hutchinson, Secretary of Health and Human Services, Tommy Thompson (National Guard escapee), Bob Barr (Representative from Georgia), Phil Gramm (Senator from Texas), Trent Lott (Senator from Mississippi), Denis Hastert (Speaker of the House), Dick Armey (former House Majority Leader), Tom ("The Exterminator") DeLay (Republican from Texas), Jeb Bush (Governor of Florida), Wayne La Pierre (Vice President of the National Rifle Association), Rush Limbaugh (drug addict), Brit Hume (Fox News), Jerry Falwell (God's Man on Earth), Supreme Court Justices Antonin Scalia and Clarence Thomas, Rudy Giuliani (former mayor), John Wayne, and Sylvester Stallone. All stayed at home during various wars to protect the land from enemies within. Many of these "domestic" heroes are right on hand to advise George when he is questioned about his heroic nude dancing on bars, offering him excuses and alibis, after which they insert that little key in his back and wind him up. Could anyone doubt that George W. is acting like a dry drunk, lying in state, when he insists that medicines imported from Canada are unsafe?

Our dry-drunk president has made public "all records" pertaining to his Air National Guard service to prove he is not a deserter; he also claims he supports community colleges, even though they need a financial cut of $230 million; likewise, youth training grants must be cut by $225 million, some 84,000 students must be deprived of their Pell Grants, and a million others should have those grants reduced. So, Pell Grants, which should be expanded, are instead being slashed. In a similarly logical vein, our bar-dancing, non-sniffer of cocaine declared that Mars is not a military objective!

When George went to honor Martin Luther King, Jr., in Atlanta, surely there was nothing amiss in using Air Force One (at $57,000 an hour); by purest coincidence, a $2,000-a-head fund-raiser happened at the same time, so, surely it was no sin to have the taxpayers foot the bill for that, too. (Aw, come on now! It was in the neighborhood!)

Surely, no reasonable person would accuse this administration of planning the invasion of Iraq long before the slaughter of 9/11. Since most of those terrorists were

Saudis, it made all kinds of sense to bomb Afghanistan and Iraq. To attack Saudi Arabia and the bin Laden family would be pure insanity.

There are filthy rumors flying about that George knows the identity of whoever leaked the name of C.I.A. agent Valerie Plame to the press. Would our fine president take part in such a felony and then perjure himself? Never! He'd dance on a bar naked rather than do such a thing.

Is it possible that Saddam Hussein sought to buy yellow cake uranium from Niger so he could make nifty little "nukular" weapons? Our acting president said it was so, and if people don't believe him, they should be detained under the provisions of the Patriot Act and sent for a long holiday in Guantanamo.

Our commander-in-chief loves our troops who fight, live, and die for "Amurika," and the fact that he plans to cut combat pay, family allowances, and death benefits doesn't mean he loves them any the less. He's not like earlier commanders-in-chief who invade families' privacy by going to soldiers' funerals. No, sir! George knows it's better to sneak coffins in under cover of darkness to save people the anguish of seeing dead kids trundled across the tarmac to the wailing of bagpipes. People should be left alone with their sorrow—that way they'll get over it faster. They should only know what real suffering is all about—when you try to stop drinking and snorting cocaine. (And what agony is worse than having your underage daughter caught buying booze?)

Of course, after remaking his life, George W. served a fine apprenticeship in death, by executing 131 criminals in Texas preparatory to killing all those "towerists" and their children in Iraq. Thankfully, the war is conducted on the cheap: a mere $750,000 a minute, or $45 million dollars an hour. On the other hand, there's no benefit in offering a dollar a day to 35,000 children abroad to save them from starvation, since they won't do a thing to earn it, and won't do a damn thing for Amurika.

Similarly, what are all those crabby old people doing, looking for bargains in medical care and drugs? Don't they know that Big Pharm, the huge pharmaceutical companies, are major donors to the Republican Party? If we don't ensure their profits, then how will we get enough cash to be reelected? Then where would Amurika be?

George is convinced that our school system is run by atheists, agnostics, vegetarians, and every other kind of Unbeliever, so it is important to revise the curriculum and set up training camps, where children will be washed in the blood of a lamb (sticky though it may be), and that they at least claim that their Savior is Jesus Christ. What nobody is telling George is that the aforesaid J. C. was a convicted felon and, had he lived in Texas under then-governor G. W. Bush, he would have been executed alongside George's other 131 victims (an all-time record for the state).

You see, George, in his frequent chats with God, learned that Jesus is God's Son, a lad he sent down to Earth to be crucified for the sins of the Bushes. Now, George W. has no sons of his own, but he is more than willing to send your sons to be killed. His generosity in this regard is reflected in his motto: *plus filius pro peccatum tuus potius:* "more sons for sins (yours, preferably)."

George neutralized any criticism of his policy by stating, in his 2000 campaign:

> "First and foremost, tell the truth. There's a lot of young people who get disillusioned when they see political figures say one thing and do another, political figures who say, 'I'm going to campaign one way,' and campaign another way, political figures who, when they take the oath of office, don't uphold the dignity and honor of the office. So, step one is to tell the truth."

So, of course, George would never lie about his insider trading of stock in Harken Energy Corporation, where he made a profit of over $800,000, just before the stock price collapsed to half its original price. Since he was merely a member of the Board of Directors, the audit committee, and the management team of Harken, how could he possibly know that the company was about to show a loss?

Likewise, his profit of $14 million on his investment in the Texas Rangers was only good business, even if taxpayers paid the bill for the new stadium.

Speaking of business, why *shouldn't* coal-fired plants be allowed to belch pollutants into the air? That stuff all drifts East anyway, and all those nitwits who insist on living in slums there should just move to a healthier climate. What the hell use are all those caribou, chomping on vegetation and taking dumps on our land? We need oil, and the Arctic is as good a place as any to drill for it. And if timber companies, to enrich their shareholders, need to eliminate those unsightly redwoods, that should indeed be their right.

Was our clueless President aware that Rumsfeld said, in September, 2002:

"There is no debate in the world as to whether [the Iraqis] have those weapons! A trained ape knows that!"

Or that the Mullah Cheney Dick said, in August 2002:

"Saddam Hussein now has Weapons of Mass Destruction. There is no doubt he is massing them to use against our allies and against us!"

Notice to Incurious George: "Step one is to tell the truth."

So, when he insisted to a Polish reporter: "We have found weapons of mass destruction and will find more as time goes on. But for those who say we haven't found the banned manufacturing devices or banned weapons, they're wrong. We found them."

Tell the truth, George, and shame the Devil!

A key thing a dry drunk needs is someone like himself to point the finger at. So, we have George W. Bush and Saddam Hussein, both of whom enjoy dressing up in uniforms. Both love their families and don't mind having folks who annoy them, such as criminals and political opponents, dispatched with extreme prejudice. They "leave no child behind"; all of them are simply *left OUT.*

A few more likenesses? Both leaders are faithful to their wives, they say. Both like guns. Neither can ride a horse. They will not tolerate disagreement from subordinates. On the other hand, Saddam seemed willing to allow his sons to die for their country, but George W. prefers that his daughters not do that. But Saddam, like George, is a dry drunk, and both are ultra-religious in the usual cruel, fundamentalist fashion, which insists that suffering be the lot of others.

George W. might have been paraphrasing Saddam, when he said:

"I'm the Commander, see? I don't need to explain why I say things. That's the interesting thing about being president. Maybe someone needs to explain to me why they say something, but I don't feel like I owe anybody an explanation."

Of course you don't, George—not the people, not the Congress, not the Supreme Court, and certainly not the people whose loved ones have been killed because *you* lie in state (and everywhere else). Go, George, and tell the family of a twenty-one-year-old boy on the threshold of life, of learning, and loving, that you don't owe them an explanation! But, let us not forget that dry drunks are angry, vengeful, spiritually bankrupt, emotionally crippled, cruel, and judgmental liars who, when caught in a lie, don't feel they owe any explanation to any other human being, no matter what the damage.

We, the American people owe an explanation to the other people of the world. To, wit: we allowed a dry drunk to become the most powerful leader in the world (he wasn't really elected, of course), and to the families of the civilians whose deaths he has caused: Sorry. To the families of the soldiers and other personnel he has sent to their deaths: Sorry. To the families of those slaughtered on the morning of 11 September, 2001: Sorry. We pledge to restore America to its place of true leadership in the world, to feed the poor, to disarm our enemies with generosity, to love and cherish all children, to safeguard the aged, and then (and only then) will we nurture all those sick and suffering citizens 'til they are well, including even dry drunks. Amen.

If You Don't Mind, It Doesn't Matter

DOES IT MATTER losing your legs?
People will always be kind,
And you need not show that you mind
As the others come in after hunting,
To gobble their waffles and eggs.

Does it matter losing your sight?
There is such splendid work for the blind,
And you need not show that you mind
As you sit on the terrace remembering,
And turning your face to the light.

Do they matter these words from the pit?
You can drink and forget and be glad,
And no one will think that you are mad
For they'll know you fought for your country,
And no one will worry a bit.

—**Siegfried Sassoon,**
World War I poem

S O DOES IT MATTER that the acting president
Blinky bin Bush and the hypocrite bin Blair of
Britain (beware the hoof of a horse, the horns of a bull,
the hiss of a snake, and the smile of an Englishman), two
of the holiest believers in Jesus Christ, Prince of Peace,
more devout in their devotion than Osama bin Laden is
to Allah—does it matter that they are the two greatest
liars of this and the last century?

DOES IT MATTER that thousands of Iraqi women
and children have been blown over the roofs of their
houses, that their limbs, heads, guts, and internal
organs have splattered the walls of their cities?

DOES IT MATTER that our acting president has
caused the United States—this glorious and wondrous land—to be hated, despised, held in contempt
by the millions to whom it had been the light of life,
the harbinger of hope?

DOES IT MATTER that our young men and women,
many of them teenagers, have been sent to die and be
so grievously wounded that many of them will never

see or walk again? Certainly the dead ones won't. Does it matter that their heads were battered with prayers, "God Bless America" and slogans, "Be all that you can be, " only to come home much less than they were when they started?

DOES IT MATTER that the acting president has attended more than a hundred fund-raisers to the cheers of his wealthy followers and received millions of dollars whilst the families of dead soldiers get $12,000, and that's it for you, kid!

DOES IT MATTER that the bodies of the dead soldiers are sneaked in under cover of night so that they are not seen by the public, certainly not the press?

DOES IT MATTER that the acting president, titular commander in chief of the armed forces, has not seen fit to attend every funeral of every young American killed for his lie? Does it matter that this liar from Texas, this self-proclaimed Christian, has not followed the injunctions of the man he claims to believe in, Jesus Christ, to visit the sick—that is, the wounded—and the grieving families?

DOES IT MATTER that his family is safe, as well as those of his cabinet and friends and Halliburton?

DOES IT MATTER that the infamous "Patriot Act" gives the likes of Blinky and Ashy and Rummy and Colin dictatorial powers over us? Does it matter that it was in March 1933 that Adolf Hitler passed the innocuous-sounding Enabling Act in response to the

Reichstag fire that was the beginning of the horrors of Nazi power over Germany and subsequently Europe?

? DOES IT MATTER that in this land of the free and home of the brave there are thousands of veterans on the streets, addicted, alcoholic and homeless and thankless?

? DOES IT MATTER that our spineless representatives with no principle voted for these acts that murder men, women, children?

? DOES IT MATTER that I have met thousands of people across the country who think they are alone in their contempt for the acting president?

So there you have it, a question of mind over matter—*if you don't mind, it doesn't matter.*

But if you do, recruit ten teenagers and ask them to vote and to each get ten other kids to join them. Be not afraid, and you only live a day at a time.

And this year we can help the reforestation of the barren lands of Texas by sending them a Bush for Christmas in the name of Jesus! So help us God.

Here are the questions:

? WHERE is Osama bin Laden?

? WHERE are the weapons of mass destruction?

? WHO sent the anthrax through the mail?

❓ HOW MANY funerals of dead soldiers has Blinky attended?

❓ HOW MANY fund-raisers did he attend?

❓ HOW MANY hospitals has Blinky visited, military or otherwise?

❓ HOW MANY Bushes have been killed, wounded, or served in the Iraqi con game?

❓ HOW MUCH did Bush know, prior to 9/11/01, about imminent terrorist attacks? (Thank you, Mr. Clarke)

P.S. On January 20, 2005, Blinky bin Bush and the Texiban gang of frauds and constitution-killers will vacate the White House and decency will be restored to us. In the meantime, God bless the world. God help America.

In War We Trust?

The killing goes on

There is nothing noble about war.

We hand out scraps of metal that have been molded into crosses, stars, and hearts, affix them to gaudy ribbons and mottoes like "honor," "distinguished," "purple," "bronze," and "silver." There are subtle distinctions, however: some people get them for killing other people; others get them for saving people; and, not that long ago, you had to be white and Christian to get any of them at all. Not entirely concealed by all this pomp and folderol is the nasty fact that to earn these baubles you have to go to war, meaning that you must face extremely frightened and hostile people who want to kill you, or, failing that, seriously wound you.

Actually, let me clarify. When they wound, rather than

kill you, it's really an accident. You, in turn, fully intend to kill these fellow human beings on the opposing side because you have learned that they are the enemy, even though you do not know their names, their ages, the color of their eyes, or even their gender. They are, simply, "the Enemy": their reasons for hating America are classified "top secret."

So you are frightened, hostile, and angry, because you have been instructed to be so. But you are buoyed by the knowledge that when you are shot through the eye or your testicles are blown away, Blinky bin Bush will blink away a tear and offer you permanent accommodations in a veterans' hospital or burial (with honors) in a military cemetery. More than most ceremonies, though, these are truly stirring, with crisply uniformed lads saluting smartly, carrying the coffins with aplomb, marching in slow step and expertly folding the flag, which is then awarded to your grieving next-of's. Talk there will be of heroes and heroism, of giving one's life for freedom and for all things American (i.e., American Airlines, American Telephone and Telegraph, American Express, Bank of America, etc.) and for things United (United Airlines, United States Trust Company, United States Steel, United Emirates, United Overseas Bank, etc.), and all those other wonderful businesses that keep the home fires burning while you go have your arse blasted to hell and beyond.

I am reminded of a sergeant named Harriman, killed in Afghanistan, whose grieving wife said he was a good husband and a good soldier, and was so glad to be in Afghanistan to be doing what he'd been training to do for sixteen years—to kill people and enable our new pals to grow poppies so that folks in our poorer neighborhoods might forget their troubles with cheap imported heroin. The good sergeant was a born-again Christian, like Blinky. His widow said her husband was a hero, even though the Bible, by which all Christians claim to be guided, says openly, "Thou Shalt Not Kill."

Perhaps that means it's OK to kill non-Americans of differing hues. I was under the impression that men and women of our nonmilitary services—the police, the fire department, and the EMS who dashed into the World Trade Center—qualified as heroes, because many of them sacrificed their lives to save others; but perhaps taking lives qualifies as heroism as well? Perhaps. Perhaps. Perhaps.

I wish people would stop moaning about the millions of jobs we've lost since September 11th, and would they just *shut up* and understand that libraries, schools and child care are lower fiscal priorities than bombs for Iraq and the war on the "Axis of Evil." Old people tire me by complaining that they can't afford food and medicine and that their senior centers are closed. Don't they know there's a war on—a war for freedom? The freedom to be old, sick, and lonely and to be able to die peacefully and in poverty. It's a war for pharmaceutical companies to be able to charge top dollar—never mind the fairer prices available from Canada. It's a war to allow us to breathe more asbestos, auto fumes, coal dust, and chemicals— any and all pollutants made by good American companies. It's a war that obliges an army of the poor to die for Blinky bin Bush and the Mullah Cheney Dick.

The Newest Evil Axis

Hoorays for more Killing?

There must be many nostalgic Germans, Italians, and Japanese who deeply resent Blinky Bush and his Texiban for placing the laurels of "Axis" on other national noggins. It was clear enough to folks living during World War II that two groups of antagonists claimed God's blessings for their side. These were the Allies, thought to be "good," being led by the likes of winsome Winnie Churchill, Uncle Joe Stalin, and dapper Franklin D. Roosevelt. Their minions were G.I. Joes, Tommies and Ivans, while the forces of the Evil Axis were directed by the raving Adolf Hitler, the cocky Benito Mussolini, and the inscrutable Emperor Hirohito.

You see, like Ken Lay, the Emperor of Enron, Hirohito was unaware of the atrocities committed in his name, so he was never tried as a war criminal. Before World War

II, an ardent Fascist, Francisco Franco of Spain, hadn't
a clue that Nazis and Fascists were testing new weapons
of mass destruction during the Spanish Civil War, so he
was spun off from the Axis. Eventually, as we all know,
the Allies were victorious in the Second War-to-end-all-
wars, because God (a Christian) listened raptly to all His
white co- religionists in England, Australia, New
Zealand, Canada, and South Africa.

The Germans and Italians, too, had their chaplains,
priests, and Gauleiters egging on their troops and praying for victory, while the Japanese perverted Buddhism
and Shinto by prodding young Kamikaze pilots into the
jihad of those days.

So, when the Blinkman looks at the Axis of Evil, does
our President see what's really there? Three countries
devastated by war, disease, and fundamentalist ideolo-
gies, with a combined population of 100 million—67 million in Iran, 23 million in Iraq, and 17 million in North
Korea, most of whom are women and children (are they
aware of being "evil"?). The Axis of Starvation is probably the only one they know about.

So, how should we handle these Axis civilians? Why,
bomb the shite out of them, of course! We've already
done that for a dozen years in Iraq, and our war
machine is all geared up for armaments to cream the
other two. Despite our enormous deficits, we have bil-
lions of dollars available for new planes and other
weapons, and, if we kill the mothers early, we will
spare them the agony of having to croon death and war
songs in the delicate ears of their children. (If we aim
well, we can kill the children too).

As our Intelligence Agencies have informed us, the Axis crowd gathers at the H.Q., "Club Evil," for dinner once a week, when guest speakers help plot and refine their terroristic activities. "Make no mistake about it" (as Blinkman and the Texiban say), terrorism is a business like any other one, so Kim Jong Il of North Korea, Muhammad Khatemi of Iran, and Saddam's surviving Baathists dine on a banquet of boiled infidels, stewed Christians, fried fundamentalists, and crock pots of compassionate conservatives, and argue over the vagaries of the terror market. Invited guests have included Meg Thatcher, the Blinkman's daddy (George Sr.), veterans of the French Algerian campaign, General William Westmoreland, Henry Kissinger, and other experienced terrorists still alive and kicking. For entertainment, there are sing-alongs with a veteran chorus composed of Arafat, Castro, and Qaddaffi, with backup from the Saudi Arabian Tabernacle Choir of 7,000 celibate princes and their 28,000 wives. Rumsfeld has been invited, but he insists he doesn't sing, preferring, rather, the whistling of bombs.

3000 Murders on Another 9/11

Violence Begets Violence

A PHOTOGRAPH OF Juliana Valentine McCourt (no relation) and her mom shows two beautiful and smiling human beings in love with life. But on September 11, 2001, Juliana, four years old, and her mom were on United Airlines Flight 175, which was deliberately smashed into the south tower of the World Trade Center, leaving a bereaved husband and father, and the rest of their loving family, trying to untangle themselves from hate, rage, thoughts of vengeance, and bewilderment. What is amazing, though, is that the family feels that the memory of these wonderful people is ill-served by the revengeful wars now underway.

Like everyone else, I've never ceased thinking about

the reasons those fanatics hijacked the planes and drove them to horrendous destruction. The short answer is that they simply hate our way of life and our beliefs, so we deserve to die. Perhaps, if we are lucky, we would see the light of Islam at death's door and say, "Oh yeah, I see it all now. Praise be to Allah," and then we, together with the assassins, would stroll hand in hand through the pearly gates. Additionally, in "martyring" themselves, they believe they are entitled to scores of virgins. Cuckoo, isn't it?

In a similar way, the ill-named "Christian Right" would refuse us any guarantee of happiness unless we accept *their* Jesus as our personal savior. Beware, all ye Jews, Catholics, Anglicans, agnostics, atheists, and liberals! The god of the Wanker in the White House is out to get you, and Jesus will crush your unbelieving skull with His cross unless you wave your arms wildly and scream that you are "saved."

Let's travel three and a half centuries back in time, to 9/11/1649, on which date the devout Christian, Oliver Cromwell, invaded the town of Drogheda, Ireland, accompanied by august Christian preachers, one of whom declared, "Cursed be he who holdeth back the sword; cursed be he that maketh not the sword stark drunk with Irish blood!" Not only men, but women and children were slaughtered because this priest, Hugh Peters, thundered: "The curse of God on those who hold their hands from slaying, while man, woman, or child of Belial remain alive." They were killed in churches, in the street, and wherever they fled; little babies were tossed into the air and impaled on soldiers' spears as they came down.

On that September 11, 1649, 3,000 Irish people of all ages died because Cromwell decreed: "This hath been a great mercy, and may all honest hearts give the glory of this to God alone, to whom indeed the praise of this mercy belongs. It was set upon some of our hearts that a great thing should be done—not by power, not by might, but by the spirit of God."

Three weeks later, the English Parliament declared a national day of thanksgiving in celebration of the slaughter, proclaiming that the House approved the murders done at Drogheda as an act of justice to them, the slaughtered ones, and an act of mercy toward others who might be warned by it. Cromwell called his soldiers "butcher saints," and said, "I thought it not right or good to restrain the soldiers from their rights of pillage or doing execution of the enemy."

Are there any lessons here for the Wanker in the White House and his cabal of Christian avengers? (Oh, there have been a few non-Christian terrorists among them too, like Perleswine and Wolfowitz).

Let's Not NIX Civil Liberties in Pursuit of Terrorism

Fearing that Fear Will Take Too Great a Toll

TO QUOTE BLINKY'S favorite line, "Make no mistake about it," he and his cabal daily promote new measures to throttle all of our liberties in the cause of Liberty. Blinky reminds me of another nincompoop, Sir Boyle Roche (1743–1807), a treacherous Irishman who, in the spirit and tradition of conservatism, sold his soul and vote for a title from the British monarch.

Roche suffered the usual conservative disease of brain damage, and his speeches revealed his nonexistent mental capacity. He once wrote a letter in which he wrote that "[Ireland] is overrun with terrorists, and we are being besieged; as I write this, I hold a pistol in one hand and a sword in the other." Get it? His quill was in his third hand?

Sir Boyle was greatly loved for his dopey speeches. Here is another of his famous howlers: "Mr. Speaker, I smell a rat; I see him forming in the air and darkening the sky; but I'll nip him in the bud."

Many of us remember the noble U.S. officer in Vietnam who declared "We have to destroy this village to save it." In a similar vein, Roche remarked: "In the great cause of civil liberty, Mr. Speaker, I should be prepared to sacrifice not only a part of our glorious constitution, but if necessary the whole of it, in order to preserve the remainder."

In the spirit of Boyle Roche, and under the guise of patriotism, our country is being engulfed in fear, goaded by our so-called leaders. Fear, especially of death, is sanitized and rarely mentioned, even by those who traffic in it professionally. We "pass away," we "pass on," we are "no longer with us." More grotesquely, the CIA practices "termination with extreme prejudice," or "permanent incapacitation." No funeral director ever includes the dreaded five-letter word in his advertising; instead, "preplanning" is advertised, as opposed to planning, a term resembling "preboarding" of airplanes (which means you get on the plane before you actually get on the plane), undertakers are there for you "in your time of need," and other such poppycock. All for the buck. Fundamentalist fanatics, Muslim and Christian, also use the language of evasion, but they don't mind giving up their lives as long they can take some of us along for the ride. (An exception is George W. Bush, who keeps himself, his family, and his Texiban far out of harm's way.) But capitalism is the most fundamental of all religions, effectively disguising its murderous terrorism by selling us tobacco, whiskey and poisonous foods. No loud explosions are caused by these fanatics, but tobacco kills nearly 5 million people worldwide every year, although there are no nicotine detectors at airport gates.

Our Big Brother Role

Puzzlement over policies that fail

SOMETHING'S ROTTEN in the world today, what with the enemies of the United States moving fluidly between continents, while hundreds of millions of democracy-minded, peace-loving people pass their every waking hour in dread of terrorists who want to kill every single one of us.

Astride the world are those who have defied every CIA effort to kill them: Fidel Castro, Mohmmar Qaddaffi, and Osama bin Laden, who seems fated to die in bed, like Stalin, Speer, and Hess.

What is astounding to me is that millions of Vietnamese remain alive today despite the Holy Axis comprised of Cardinal "Frannie" Spellman (as he was known to altar boys), Richard Nixon, Roy Cohn, Alexander Haig, Henry Kissinger, and Robert MacNamara, who wanted to nuke 'em all. Equally strange that most of the almost 23 million Iraqis still survive after two wars against them and the cruel sanctions initiated by Big Blinky bin Bush in the early '90s. The slower form of killing, the sanctions, had managed to increase the infant mortality rate by a mere 250 percent. Only one in eight children now dies before turning one; we might move to ease their suffering by making sure that four out of eight die before their first birthday. Additionally, only another 120 out of every thousand die before the age of 5—a shocking percentage, revealing our carelessness in allowing so many of them to live. From 1975 to 1990, the child mortality rate fell dramatically in Iraq, but then along came Kuwait, which was stealing Iraqi oil by slant drilling. Enter the United States, with its sanctions, and suddenly Saddam Hussein had a powerful partner in wiping out his own people. This still wasn't good enough. With the American occupation, hospitals in Iraq occasionally have clean water, despite the fact that our current commander-in-chief/draft dodger continued the destruction of water filtration plants.

Water is available in 51 percent of urban areas in Iraq, and 33 percent of rural ones. Raw sewage still flows in streets and homes at times. Typhoid, cholera, and other epidemics still break out, thanks to effects of the war in Iraq and conditions left over from the sanctions. Only 20 percent of Iraqi women suffer from anemia. Can't we go for 100 percent? A superpower with a super-idiot leading it will not balk at any means of punishing a civilian population. The constitution of the World Health Organization sez:

> "The enjoyment of the highest standard of health is one of the fundamental rights of every human being without distinction of race, religion, political belief, economic or social condition."

Also, the Universal Declaration of Human Rights sez:

> "Everyone has the right to a standard of living adequate for self and family, including food, shelter and medical services, and the right to security in the event of sickness . . . , widowhood, old age, or other lack of livelihood in circumstances beyond his control."

Likewise, the Geneva Convention insists:

> "(1) Starvation of civilians as a method of warfare is prohibited; (2) It is prohibited to destroy objects necessary for the production of foodstuffs or drinking-water installations, whether to starve out civilians or cause them to move away or for any other motive."

Since we as a nation lay formal claim to God's Blessings Upon America, we know that God is not free to bless any other place or people on earth, so we are at liberty to ignore all protocols, covenants, treaties, agreements, or the rights of ordinary humans who live elsewhere, 'coz God obviously does not like them. They are deficient in the noble feelings and values that the bin Bushes (and the rest of us) have. Recall that General Westmoreland years ago insisted that the Vietnamese do not feel the loss of life or grieve as we do.

So, it is time to stop cocking about and get serious about the business of killing all Iraqis.

Bush
and the
Evil
That
Men Do

For some years now, I've been reflecting on the nature of Evil, and its many origins and guises. It's usually where you least expect it, dressed in grey or blue business suits and red ties, or speaking with a phony Texas drawl, smiling, looking earnest, and mimicking an ordinary good ol' boy who likes nothing better but to laze on the front porch, munch on a piece of straw, and once in a while do a Lizzie Borden on a pile of innocent logs.

George Wanker bin Bush (our beloved Blinky), personifies Evil. His favorite philosopher, he claims, is Jesus Christ, a man who would recoil at killing little children. Indeed, He insisted: "Suffer the little children to come unto me, and forbid them not, for such is the kingdom of God."

Former priests who molest little children are put in jail, whilst those who kill them are rewarded as defenders of freedom. In what way is it worse to molest a child than to kill her? Every day, young Americans kill and get killed on the orders of their Commander-in-Chief, who has fooled them into believing that they are doing God's work. Now hear this! As Blaise Pascal once said: "Men never do evil so completely and cheerfully as when they do it from religious conviction." Thus, everything the Wanker does is evil. Since he stole the election, he has lied, he has stolen from the poor and given to the rich, he has deprived people of their constitutional rights, and never once has he owned up to the damage done to his brain by narcotics. He has allowed corporate officers to steal investors' money, as he once reaped an enormous profit by building his Texas baseball stadium at public expense. He and his family have been business partners with Saudi Arabia (including the bin Laden family), a cruel and repressive monarchy that executes people for the slightest offense.

Yes, Blinky is evil in everything he does and touches. Has he once ever come out against taxing Social Security benefits for the elderly poor and infirm? Has he ever made a move against taxing unemployment benefits? Has he done anything to assist poor people in going to college? Has he done anything to get medical benefits and medicines for poor people?

When did he ever say that pay for armed services personnel should not be taxed? Never. On the contrary,

Wanker's administration wants to remove the current $225 a month combat ("imminent danger") pay, and to eliminate the $250-a-month separation allowance given a family to cope while their breadwinner is at war. (This last bit of thievery was dropped, as it looked "unpatriotic" to Bush's spinmeisters.)

Since the forced departure of Christie Whitman as head of the E.P.A., every polluting industry in the nation has been uncorking its poison-spewing chimneys, while childhood asthma rates continue to soar. Mercury from coal-fired plants has polluted the seas, so the tunafish sandwich in the kids' lunchbox is poison now. Blinky, that's not what Christ meant by "Suffer the little children." He said don't molest them, poison them, or kill them. "Suffer them" doesn't mean "make 'em suffer."

My Personal Alphabet

OCCASIONALLY, one of my highly intelligent conservative critics will refer to me as a boring, self-righteous old crank. One of them commented on my literacy, suggesting that I practice the alphabet instead of writing. Since most of my antagonists are unfamiliar with the alphabet, I'm going to recite it right now.

This will be an especially short chapter, since conservatives (the ones most in need of this information) have a miniscule attention span, and they much prefer to hear that brilliant, wildly scintillating and deeply intellectual epigrammatist, sophisticate, and plunderer of the White House, George Wanker Bush, explain why he is wrecking the world and destroying our liberties. So, here's an alphabetical listing of terms useful for describing this thief of our rights:

BUSH LIES IN STATE

A Asinine

B Banal Blinky

C Cocaloru

D Dunderhead

E Evader

F Fraud, Foul

G Goddam Liar

H Hypocrite

I Inclined to Idiocy

J Jejune

K Know Nothing

L Liar

M Marrowless

N Numbskull

O Oily

P Puppet, Perjurer

Q Quill Pig

R Rodent

S Stench

T Taradiddler

U	Usurper
V	Vermicious
W	Wanker, Whore
X	Xloid
Y	Yahoo
Z	Zoril

So, there you have your wish, dear sycophant of Bush. I trust you will be able to find someone to read it to you.

Intriguing Answer from bin Laden

(and a War Whoop from the Militarists)

Q. *Mr. bin Laden, what is your opinion of George W. Bush?*

A. *Praise be to Allah, he has been the answer to my prayers. First, that secular despot Saddam has been removed from power. The chances that the Shiite mullahs, with my help, can now establish a true Islamic state in Iraq have greatly improved.*

Second, our recruitment problems are over. Would-be martyrs abound. Third, he has provided them with ample targets on the ground in an Arab country. Fourth, he has made it clear to the 1.5 billion Muslims that America is the number one enemy of Islam. Even in infidel countries, many consider him to be the world's greatest threat to peace. Finally, he has led America into a color-coded frenzy of fear wondering what we will do next. How gratifying!

These have been goals of Al Qaeda and they could not have been accomplished without him. Granted, he has upset our training program and has made it more difficult for us to transfer funds to our operatives, but on balance he has been a great boon to our cause. God willing (his and mine), he will be with us for four more years!

A FLIGHT OF FANCY this (maybe), but these are ripe days for Osama as well as Blinky Bush and his pals. In fact, there's no better time to be a greedy arms maker than the present. The U.S. already violates all nuclear arms treaties, new weapons races are under way, and it's whoopee time for militarists throughout the world.

Any objections? Well, Blinky has an answer to all of them. It's labelled . . . *education.* And here's the deal: get all the children into school, every day of the year, summer included. Indoctrination guaranteed (this is not *education* at all, but *groupthink.* Thank you, George Orwell). Specifications for new desks are being developed, as they need to be bigger than the ones students used to take shelter under during the Cold War.

Many people still remember the futile gestures of drilling students to dive under their desks in preparation for nuclear attacks. (A metal dog tag was thoughtfully provided, in the event that their parents had to identify their blackened "cremains.") But Blinky shrewdly recognized that a school desk offers the best defense against an atomic bomb (especially if you also have an umbrella), so new and reinforced ones will be ordered, bringing great wealth to school suppliers as well as umbrella makers. (The Bushites still don't realize that when Numbnuts Reagan floated his missile defense idea, he wasn't referring literally to "umbrellas.")

Of course, even if no attack ever comes, fear is the best way to keep people from asking embarrassing questions.

Prior to September 11, and after Pearl Harbor, the worst attack on the United States came from a trained Army man who claimed to be a patriot and (in his diseased brain) a highly original thinker. The U.S. Army had trained him to kill, so his skill was applied to 168 men, women and children, all for the glory of America. Oddly though, instead of getting a medal for trying to preserve the Constitution, Timothy McVeigh was sentenced to death, this brave soldier who followed his conscience by killing Iraqis and Oklahomans. His only regret was that he had only 168 lives of other people to give for his country.

Others among the good friends of America, Noriega of Panama, Saddam of Iraq, Somoza of Nicaragua, and Pahlavi, the Shah of Iran, discovered too late the perils of killing and doing business with the United States. Some spider species kill their mates immediately after the act of love.

Oh, the Things Bad Shellfish Can Teach You

A conversation with the Almighty about current events.

THE ONLY PEOPLE in the United States qualified to say "My God" are the Rev. Pat Robertson, Karl Rove, and his puppet, Blinky bin Bush. By a prior arrangement with Bill Gates, Pat Robertson was able to contact God on the Internet, much to Al Gore's chagrin, and they have been talking and talking and talking. We have to thank the Rev. Robertson for conveying God's will to us. If all America will obey this Divine One, He will answer our prayers.

He will tell everyone the lottery number to bet on, the winning horse in the Kentucky Derby, how to avoid Martha Stewart's fate, the winner of the World Series, and which team will win the Super Bowl. He will also assure us that only sinners are killed in Iraq and in any future terrorist attacks.

So, there you have it. You will wonder how I got this information. Well, I got a touch of food poisoning, and in the course of my puking and high fever, God decided to talk to me.

The first thing God said to me was, "I dislike name droppers." And furthermore, He said, "I have been occupying the Lincoln Bedroom at the White House, and, boy, could I dish some dirt about what goes on there."

At times, the phone connection to Heaven was interrupted by mass call-ins from fundamentalists, reserving places on the Right Hand of Himself. (Hint to travelers who may be destined for Paradise: reserve on the left-hand side of God, since it's less crowded and all the interesting people are there, though most of the truly colorful people are down below, in that place where you can light your pipe with your finger. (As Dorothy Parker once said, "Give me heaven for the comfort and hell for the company.")

But I digress. During our conversations, God confided to me that He really admires Attorney General Ashcroft, as John covered up that tit on the statue of Justice, thus saving America from aggravated prurience. In addition, John loves Jesus more than his own wife, even though

Jesus had plenty of hang-ups, never married, and hung out with twelve other guys, forming the unlucky thirteen.

God related to me that He is a bit pissed off at Blinky bin Bush's claim that Jesus is his favorite philosopher as, sez He, "Whose son is Jesus anyway? And who sent Him to earth to be crucified?"

He said He was planning to send Jesus to Texas to be executed, but, as Blinky had already presided over the deaths of 131 people there (not to mention 11,000 Iraqis civilians and 750-plus American soldiers), He thought He'd get Jesus tried for sedition and crucified right away, to cash in on early publicity and get the jump on capital punishment. Besides, making the Sign of the Cross is much simpler than attempting the Sign of the Electric Chair or the Sign of the Lethal Injection.

The next time God called, 'twas on the cell phone, when He asked me to meet Him in person, which I did in the back of a strip club on Staten Island. He said no one would expect to find God in such a joint, and no one would expect to find nudity on Staten Island, as sins of the flesh are outlawed there.

He described the prayer breakfasts at the White House, where He feels awkward, because, Himself being the only God, He has no one to pray to (He is, after all, The Boss, despite Bruce Springsteen's claim to the title). Blinky bin Bush hopes to get God to tender his resignation, offering Him a graceful exit, saying "He can spend more time with His Family" and "He would have time to do volunteer social work with condemned prisoners on Death Row in Texas."

In the meantime, the Bushites have agreed that "God

Bless America!" will be emblazoned on one side of the American flag, while the other will read "To Hell With the Rest of the World." All Jews, Muslims, agnostics, atheists, socialists, vegetarians, and any Democratic candidate for the presidency will be hauled off to Texas for re-education and indoctrination in the prime principles of conservatism (in preparation, ninety percent of their brains will be surgically removed). Furthermore, all poor people will be obliged to donate organs—eyes, lungs, hearts, kidneys, livers—to the wealthiest American families, as these are the only ones who do anything at all for this country.

All banks will be required to post signs that say "Jesus Saves," and all bank tellers must be Born Again and ordained as Ministers of Money. 'Twas then that God said we should go and watch the girls strip, as He'd forgotten female anatomy, since it was so long ago that he originated the species by making Eve.

I had one more call from God, in which He joyously told me that he had given vast sums of money to Satan to buy fuel for the fires of Hell, as that's where Blinky and his thugs are destined to go—on God's order. As God pronounced, "No More Years" for those who would destroy democracy.

Trading
with the
Enemy

And other follies "under God" and under Bush

AN EXCELLENT BULLETIN called *Public Citizen News* recently ran some juicy stuff. It appears that almost any activity can be sanctioned as long as the ultimate goals are money making and "trade." Nevertheless, 62 companies were fined a total of the enormous sum of $1.4 million by the U.S. Treasury Office of Foreign Assets Control, for "trading with the enemy." $1.4 million! Wow! We spend over thirty times that much ($45 million) per HOUR for so-called "defense," so the fine would have paid for about two minutes of national defense against an attack by whom? Monaco?

Here's a partial breakdown of the fines:

$ Chevron Texaco, $14,000, for trading with Iraq;

$ Fleet Bank, $41,000, for trading with Iran;

$ Exxon Mobil, $50,000, for trading with Sudan;

$ New York Yankees, $75,000, for trading with Cuba;

$ Wal-Mart, $50,000, for trading with Cuba;

$ ESPN, $40,000, for trading with Cuba;

$ Caterpillar, $18,000, for trading with Cuba.

Now, the government was reluctant to reveal these and other figures, until *Public Citizen* lawyer, Michael Tanerly, sued under the Freedom of Information Act. Lovely stuff. Now, *Public Citizen* is also suing because Blinky bin Bush and the Texiban are trying ever harder to hide their misdeeds from our eyes. One of Johnny Ashcroft's earliest memos instructed all government agencies to use every legal maneuver at their disposal to frustrate Freedom of Information requests. Now we will never be able to learn what deal Cheney Dick cut with Enron to soak California citizens with astronomical energy costs. Forever hidden from public view will be the sneaky process by which the same V.P., former C.E.O. of Halliburton, got the Department of Defense to award a noncompetitive bid of $7 billion to that company for contracts in Iraq.

Now, it is impossible that this contract happened because Cheney Dick is on the Halliburton payroll. His compensation is, after all, "deferred"—to the tune of millions of dollars a year, whilst he remains vice president.

"Have a heart," as the transplant surgeon said. There is so much cynicism about! Is it conceivable that Blinky has burned the 1,600 pages of Blinky Senior's involvement in the Iran/Contra perjury and murder scandal for any reason other than national security? Will we ever discover what happened to Blinky's coke dealer at Yale, or where Blinky was when he "absented" himself (without leave) for a year from the Texas Air National Guard (this latter being done in time of war, and thus, technically a capital offense)? Not bloody likely, sis.

Unless, of course, *Public Citizen* succeeds in its mission to wring the truth out of the biggest bunch of neo-fascists this country has seen since the era of that jolly Irishman, Senator Joe McCarthy, and his creepy acolyte, Roy Cohn.

Blinky displayed typical arrogance of power in his interviews with Bob Woodward: "I'm the Commander, see . . . I do not need to explain why I say things." What an interesting view of the President as Thug! The paraphrase of Edward G. Robinson is almost exact: "I'm Rico. I'm the boss, see . . . I don't owe anyone nuttin'." Of course, since Blinky wasn't *really* elected (he lost by half a million votes), he doesn't owe us anything in the way of explanation (except, maybe to his mom, who had a breech birth, so he came out with both feet in his mouth).

We do know, of course, why thousands of American teenagers are bleeding and dying in Iraq and Afghanistan—for the rights to be unemployed, to swill Coca-Cola, to chomp McDonald's fat-filled fries (sorry, "freedom fries"), to wave the flag, to extoll the lunatic Christian right, and for the red, white and blue fabric that is under God, keeping His bottom warm.

Cynics among us might insist that it's all about oil. *Tut tut.* Do you imagine we'd send our boys and girls to suffer and die just for the black sticky stuff? Unthinkable! Though Blinky and his family and cabinet, as well as the Congress, have no kids in the armed services, they are willing to sacrifice lives and limbs of working people for that Mideast petrochemical. Blinky made a quick Thanksgiving visit to pep talk our kids into battle, but he doesn't attend any of their funerals. That would get bad press.

Why
the
Politicians
Starve
the
Schools

Uneducated electorate tolerates lies and wars

NUMEROUS AWARDS are given to the wonderful people involved in teaching, as well as administrators, parents, assistants, and other assorted bods who do the tedious work. Of course, all people involved in education have one thing in common: as long as they work in this noble arena, they will never grow rich, very few will achieve fame, and most will live out their final years on paltry pensions. Perhaps they will be remembered by grateful students somewhere whose lives were touched by them. But because they do not toss balls around the field, nor do they chew things, spit, or paw the ground like frustrated bulls, or scratch their testicles, the roar of a crowd will never reach their ears. The educator who appears on stage, screen or television and admits to being a teacher must be prepared for the suppressed yawn, and there will be no whipping out of checkbooks and golden fountain pens to sign them to long-term, multimillion dollar contracts for only a few weeks of work per year.

So, when war is declared, and the gigantic bills for mass destruction come due, who has to pay them? The children now in school, that's who, because the money that goes toward destruction and killing is subtracted from education, and the desolation is universal. Those in power yap about "leaving no child behind," since they are our future and our hope.

Let me advise the pious yappers—lying swine that they are—that there will be no future as things are going, and I DO care about children, mine and everyone else's, so I don't want to hear any lying about what awaits them.

So what's the deal? Here it is: no politicians, Democrats or Republicans really want children to be educated, because education teaches people to think for themselves—to seek knowledge, to apply their judgment, to make decisions, and to leave this earth a better place than when they entered it.

So what do the lying swine want? It's war they want, so they can appear to ride in on mythical white horses to save us from evil beings like Osama and Saddam. Note this analogy: how often do we read of volunteer fireman around the country who set fires so they can have opportunities to become heroes? The question we must ask is, "*Cui bono?*" Who benefits?

If we had an educated voting populace, lying politicians would have to spend their lives screwing each other instead of the decent but ill-read people in this country. Educated voters would never succumb to war fever, flag-waving hysteria, or the illiterate nonsense of that hemorrhoid in the White House, George Wanker Bush.

Of course, for education to be any good, it has to be leavened with ethics, morality, and spirituality (not to mention good examples). Crime must be kept out of the schools, and every teacher should be paid as highly as a Senator, but if he or she becomes an administrator, the salary should be reduced. The Chancellor should have to pay to hold the job. The education budget should be 100 times that of the military, whose generals and admirals should have to pay to wear uniforms with all those silly ribbons on their chests.

An acclaimed children's writer told me that in her talks on bullying in the classroom her prime example of a bully is the White House Wanker.

Who Says None Dare Call It Treason?

Welcome to the era of compassionate treason

PERHAPS THE MOST distinguished conservative in our history was Benedict Arnold. In fact, I find it difficult to find traitors who are not conservative. The reason is, of course, that conservatives value material goods above any principle. On any day of the week you can hear or read them yowling on radio talk shows and in yellow journals, moaning about taxes.

They yap about "property values," when, in fact they are concerned about monetary investments only. Conservative traitors, lords of the land, include jumped-up sons of bitches who harass and worry elderly citizens with threats of eviction and rent hikes. Conservatism is by its very nature treacherous, in that it betrays the very principles on which America is founded. English King George the Mad, Number 3, pronounced: "I desire what is good; therefore everyone who does not agree with me is a traitor." Jump ahead to the reign of George W. (Blinky) bin Bush, who declared that he who is not with America is with the terrorists. By that, he means that everyone who opposes his lust for power and his royal designs such as the terroristic Patriot Act is un-American.

"A conservative government is an organized hypocrisy," said Benjamin Disraeli in 1845. With this definition in hand, let us examine what we have in government this day: "compassionate conservatives." Would they say one thing and do another? Would they rip away money from poor people and give it to military contractors? Would they demolish the sacred barrier that exists between church and state? Would they savagely despoil the purity of the Arctic for oil? Would they lie about the existence of weapons of mass destruction abroad? Would they take blood money from cigarette manufacturers? Cigarettes are weapons of mass destruction, so why not bomb them too?

And, above all, do they believe in JEE-SUSS? That's how most of them say it. Eyes must be screwed tightly shut so as to obliterate images of the outside world, the jaw must be thrust forward, and the neck held so rigidly as to produce tremors, as the name JEE-SUSS is forced from the lips in a frenzy like that of a loony Crusader with a broadsword attacking an infidel Muslim.

Yes, but this JEE-SUSS was in truth a lawbreaker, sentenced to death by the capital punishment boyos of his day—conservatives all of them. Phillip Brooke wrote: "In the best sense of the word, Jesus was a radical. His religion has been so long identified with conservatism, often with conservatism of the most obstinate and unyielding sort—that it is almost startling to remember that all the conservative forces of his time were arrayed against him! It was the young, free, restless, sanguine, progressive part of the people who flocked to him."

There is much talk among the ultra-religious about either JEE-SUSS or some other Messiah hopping back onto Planet Earth. If He (or She) is listening, please accept my advice: "Don't do it. If you arrive in Utah, they'll execute you by firing squad; in Florida, in the electric chair; New York ditto; elsewhere, via lethal injection. At the very least, you'll get shipped to Guantanamo Bay."

Anyway, I've wandered off my original premise about conservatives and traitors being one and the same. Benedict Arnold adored royalty and despised common people, so he hoped that with the Brits in firm control of the colonies, he would be crowned King Benedict the First. He failed, but little did he guess, that eventually an American royal line would spring from dirt, manure, saplings, shrubs, and Bushes, all eagerly and religiously betraying everything the Founding Daddy-Os stood for.

Guess what? Now we have the Bush Dynasty (don't miss Kevin Phllips' best seller, *American Dynasty*).

Ralph Waldo Emerson had another enlightening comment: "Conservatism is merely defensive of property. It vindicates no right, it aspires to no real good, it brands no crime, it proposes no generous policy, it does not build nor write nor cherish the arts, nor establish schools nor encourage science nor emancipate the slave nor befriend the poor or the Indian or the emigrant."

God bless the world. God help America.

Of the United Nations, the President, the War(s)

Sacrifices must be made— but of whom?

Not long after the Republican presidential convention, 'twill be time again when the headgear comes to town, accompanied by heads of state, stateless heads, and empty heads (some of them) for the opening of the U.N. General Assembly. You'll see kepis, burnooses (is the plural "burneese"?), tams, fezzes (or is it "fezi"?), turbans, fedoras, caps, skullcaps, yarmulkes, helmets, top hats, berets, and scrambled-egg military hats. Almost

200 countries present themselves as "united nations," but, of course, we know better.

That crowd of gangsters, tipsters, idealists, ideologues, visionaries, humanitarians, assholes, dictators, tyrants, and vassals gather each fall in our great City of New York to take part in a grand effort at what may be humankind's only hope of survival. It's astounding that this organization has lasted for almost sixty years, despite the efforts of assorted yahoos to destroy it, debase it, or ignore it. The light of truth and compassion that led to its founding still penetrates the gloom of those who show contempt for the organization that, however flawed, has a truly noble mission.

Last year, that disgusting little man, Blinky bin Bush, aka "Wanker," with all the dignity of a deballed rooster, strode to the podium in the famed building on the East River and hectored the collected dignitaries about his great achievements, without their help or approval, in bringing peace and democracy to Iraq. Despite his brilliant fight against "towerism" and "nukular" proliferation (U.N. translators had a tough time with this language), he has made a mess, and now he wants (as does any spoiled rich kid) to have the servants get the ka-ka out of his pants and wipe his bottom clean. Otherwise, he will stamp his foot and scream and scream and scream, 'til Mommy comes and fires the whole bloody lot of them.

Nowhere in his petulant, self-praising tirade did the Wanker mention the desperate state of our cities, with their deteriorating schools, overtaxed soup kitchens, and bursting shelters for the homeless. No mention of our record-breaking budget deficit, nor the massive job losses, unsurpassed since the Great Depression. Every year, five million children die worldwide for want of food and water.

No, sir! The fight on "towerism" must be fought and won, no matter how many of your sons and daughters have to die in Afghanistan and Iraq. Sacrifices must be made, and, so long as the daughters of the Acting President, Cheney Dick, the cabinet and the Congress remain safe at home, 'twill be done.

Our huge inventory of body bags (manufactured from oil by-products, and costing around $32—the same as a barrel of sweet crude oil) is being put to good use. Within them, twenty-somethings are packaged and delivered to families who can only be proud that their son, daughter, wife, husband, or brother died for freedom. Since the United States restored Iraq to "freedom" (and found all those weapons of mass destruction), only **eight hundred** soldiers have died, with many thousands more wounded as the results of hostile and nonhostile action.

Most people's image of a wound comes from draft-dodger John Wayne's films, where something strikes his shoulder and he transfers his revolver and keeps bravely shooting with the other hand. The reality is far different: faces are blown away, arms and legs mangled and amputated, and (whisper, whisper) many a young man will never father a child because his genitalia were shattered on the Iraqi desert.

In the midst of this mess, we still have to ask:

Where are those weapons of mass destruction?

Who sent anthrax through the mail?

Where is Osama bin Laden?

How does Rummy spend his $45 million every hour of the day?

A Grand Time We Live in

But also a time of strange priorities

THE FINANCIAL LOSS to New York City as a result of the slaughter and damage of September 11, 2001, has been estimated at $83 billion dollars. If Bill Gates were to write a check for that amount, he would be left with a mere $17 billion dollars and, as my friend Joe Hayes would say, "my heart pumps piss for him" in sympathy with that degree of penury. (Sorry—Bill's wealth recently plummeted to a mere $31 billion, so we can't be too hard on the poor guy: see "Bill Gates' Net Worth" page on the Web).

And isn't it a grand time we live in? Back in the '90s, we had Bill Clinton and his boys shouting and strategizing that "It's the economy, stupid!" But the Republicans, who all became oral surgeons overnight, responded, "No, no, it's fellatio"—a word which needed to be defined for them by Bob Grant. But as Sidney Webb, co-founder of the Fabian Society, did say, "The hungry man's revolution stops at the baker's shop, and so now nobody give's a fiddler's fart about the Clinton White House's open mouth policy. So now, it is once again "the economy, stupid!," but we have been bamboozled by Blinky and his thugs into believing that the entire world is in thrall to terrorism.

Under this pall of fear, the nation is being robbed so that large corporations can fill their coffers, corrupt our public servants, and exert ever more control over our lives. Mussolini, who invented the term "Fascism," defined it as a *stato corporativo*, or "corporate state," exactly the sort of system we have now in the United States. The main priority now is to build armies and armaments (cruise missiles and other high-tech weapons cost a million dollars apiece), send hundreds of thousands of soldiers abroad to be killed or maimed while firing (sorry, "downsizing") millions of people back home.

Here's just one modest example of how the corporate state policy brings grief to ordinary people. Old and infirm people throughout the nation are rotting away for want of direct care or nursing care, since the people who wash and clean those folks with disabilities are paid a pittance because they do not flash in the headlines like our war leaders and kids in uniform, who make explosions and kill while being killed. You see, direct care workers from voluntary agencies get, on average, about $21,000 per annum—and that includes overtime. In New York

City, the wages are as low as $7.85 an hour before taxes, and that, dear friends, works out to $314 per week. (This is in a city where a shabby shoebox, now called a "studio apartment," can cost $1,400 a month; transit fare will run you at least four dollars a day; and may your Higher Power help you if you ever care to take your beloved to a movie, at $10.50 a head.)

It's even worse outside the cities, where caretakers of people with disabilities are paid a mere $6.75 an hour, and things have gotten so bad that many of these workers who have children must apply for Medicaid, food stamps, subsidized housing, and charitable help. At any given time, the manpower shortage is so severe that new residences cannot be opened and in existing ones the meager staff are miserably overworked.

So what would it take to ensure that those people who nurture and safeguard our neediest citizens can live decent and dignified lives? In New York City, $17.50 an hour for a forty-hour week is what's necessary and a shade less in other areas of the nation. So, one cruise missile would pay for 30 workers for a year; 10 of them would finance 300 caretakers, and so on.

There are scores of voluntary agencies, but during this time of financial shortfalls, due to cuts in charitable contributions and government aid, workers are leaving the field for jobs that pay even slightly more, because they're so close to the margin of survival.

If Blinky and the Cheney Dick can provide endless corporate welfare to GE, IBM, Halliburton, Enron, and other of their rich friends, surely they can squeeze out a bit for the most helpless among us, who work hard but have no lobbyists on their side.

Bush-Style Business

(at last, I've seen the light!)

I fear I have been beastly to the Texiban, and with the endearing and gentle rebukes I have received, these Irish eyes are not smiling but misting over with gratitude to the thoughtful Bushies, who chide me, using such lovely and sensitive language as "jerk," "asshole," "fool," "commie," "prick," "schmuck," and "traitor." But harken! The scales have dropped from the baby blue orbs, and finally I see the light. I now march in lockstep with the Commander-in-Thief on the road to righteousness and propriety, and, as we advance together, we the bin Bushes, and the Mullah Cheney Dicks, we trumpet our new anthem, a specially altered version of Noel Coward's song, "Let's Don't Be Beastly!" So, all together now: here goes!

We must be just
And win their love and trust
And in addition we must
Be wise
And ask the corporate heads to join our
Hands to aid them.
That would be a wonderful surprise.
For many years
They've been in a flood of tears
Because the poor little dears
Have been so wronged and only longed
To cheat the world,
Deplete the world,
And beat
The world to blazes.
This is the moment when we
Ought to sing their praises.

All of the bin Bush family business and government dealings have been honest and above-board; even when big Blinky headed the CIA, no assassination or drug deal was finalized unless he had consulted at least one other person (even though she was his own wife).

And if anyone thinks that brother Neil bin Bush was guilty of wrongdoing in that Silverado Bank scandal, shame on you! The savings and loan bailout was a patriotic duty, for which every citizen should be grateful and willing to pay. After all, the banks did the right thing by redistributing wealth upward.

Likewise, when the Harken Oil Company got an enormous Bahrain oil-drilling deal without competitive bidding, there was no suspicion that Blinky, the soon-to-be President's son, a $120,000- a-year consultant, had anything to do with it. When the company lent said son $150,000 and then forgave the loan, why was that anything but normal business procedure?

Now we all know that Blinky and all the bin Bushes oppose sin, immorality, and those very bad people who steal from the rich, so when the SEC—which was then headed by Richard Breedlove (who had been deputy counsel to V.P. Blinky bin Bush, Sr.), and the general counsel to the same SEC was James Doty (the same lawyer who had helped Blinky buy the Texas Rangers)— decided to make no investigation of insider trading, surely you can't suspect it was due to family and business connections. Good heavens, no! And even the later SEC boss, Harvey Pitt, insisted that the SEC should become ever warmer and friendlier to corporate interests. Compare: bin Laden's attack cost America about $100 billion (not counting the lives of those slaughtered). But the corporate attack on America has cost upward of $600 billion since Blinky's non-election (not counting hundreds of thousands of ruined lives).

In 1904, a famed Tammany operative, also named George W. (Plunkitt) remarked, "Everybody is talkin' these days about Tammany men growin' rich on graft, but nobody thinks of drawin' the distinction between honest graft and dishonest graft. There's all the difference in the world between the two. Yes, many of our men have grown rich in politics. I have myself. I've made a big fortune out of the game, and I'm gettin' richer every day, but I've not gone in for dishonest graft – blackmailin' gamblers, saloon-keepers, disorderly people, etc.—and neither has any of the men who have made big fortunes in politics."

"There's an honest graft, and I'm an example of how it works. I might sum up the whole thing by sayin': 'I seen my opportunities and I took 'em.'"

Jump to 1989, and the George W. of this era (our very own Blinky) echoes Plunkitt: "I saw a business opportunity, and I seized it." He also persuaded the city of Arlington, TX, to raise taxes for a stadium, and when the Rangers were sold, G.W. made $14 million on his half-a-million dollar investment, but all the taxpayers got were higher ticket prices in their new stadium. The Mullah Cheney Dick has had a lot of bad press from his dealings with Halliburton and Arthur Andersen. Meanwhile, I have it on bad authority that Big Blinky intends to refuse his pension and his Secret Service protection, and that Jeb of Florida will refuse his salary, and Blinky plans to refund his Presidential stipend plus all the money he skimmed from insider trading at Harken. Silverado bin Bush brother is also paying back the fleeced S & L depositors. Mullah Cheney Dick will offer his services for zip, as will all the Cabinet members. If you believe that, you'll easily be convinced that Blinky never sniffed cocaine.

Big Business Is Innocent

Bush and Crooked Corporations? No connection!

IT'S AN ABSOLUTE DISGRACE that accusations still linger that Blinky Bush and Cheney Dick are linked financially to corporations that donate huge sums to their election campaigns. It is well recognized that all American businesses are honest, moral, God-fearing entities that donate money, never wishing anything in return. In fact, were it not for laws forcing them to reveal their identities, they would give much more, and do so anonymously. However, there is an absurd idea that has taken root in the national psyche that the Captains of Industry are in business solely to make money for the officers and shareholders in their corporations.

Let us examine the record. It is well recognized that businesses are hamstrung by federal, state, and city governments, all conspiring to tax them for the governments' own selfish ends. Moreover, said corporations are also vilified and harassed by beetle-browed thugs wanting only to extract more money and fewer hours for their workers, who also have the cheek, the nerve, and the gall to expect insurance against illness and accidents on the job. Then, they expect that after a mere 30 or 40 years on the job, to be awarded a pension so that they can live out their lives in slothful and undeserved comfort.

Yet more burdens encumber our beloved business community. In their efforts to sweeten life for the consumer, they often slip some unlisted substances, like sugar, into products, only to have those damn diabetics make a big fuss. Then we have those fanatical critics of alcohol, who want distillers to list the ingredients in the booze. If that were done, people might cut back on their drinking, and then where would we be?

Then we have those pesky people who go around yelling that smoking tobacco causes lung cancer and lip cancer, that secondhand smoke also causes emphysema and asthma (especially in young children), and that tobacco addiction is harder to kick than either crack or heroin. How ridiculous! We all saw top executives of the tobacco companies swear under oath (whilst I swore under my breath) that tobacco is harmless. For God's sake, hadn't Ronnie Reagan made commercials for Chesterfields? (They purified your lungs so you wouldn't catch cold.) Hadn't John Wayne, Humphrey Bogart, Audie Murphy, Bette Davis and other all-American types been heavy smokers?

There is no convincing proof that auto emissions and coal-fired plants raise pollution levels or fat-soaked fried food harms children. It's only those self-appointed moralists and killjoys like Ralph Nader, who should check into monastaries, who go about nitpicking about good American companies, the same ones that create jobs in Indonesia, Mexico, China, and South America, thereby maximizing productivity so that cheap goods can be available to unemployed workers in the U.S. What's wrong with that?

Likewise, if schools are failing and sickness goes untreated across the land, it's hardly the responsibility of corporations. Already they're overburdened with political donations, and with taxes, which they sometimes pay. Add to that lobbyists' fees, power lunches, dinners, golf, tennis, the cost of joining Blinky's team ($1 million), the burdens of offshore banking, and the upkeep of private planes and and ocean-going yachts.

So, why was there any cause for suspicion when the chief lobbyist for Enron gave $50,000 to Blinky for his gubernatorial inauguration party? He stated: "We clearly never expect to receive anything other than good government as a result of any kind of contribution we make." It's a mere coincidence, then, that Blinky pushed through a bill, much favored by Enron, deregulating electricity. California was nearly bankrupted by this little maneuver.

So, dear citizens, please buy flags and SUVs, eat more, consume more, and cut down more trees. What's a few PCBs in our rivers? Asthma results from people living in poor neighborhoods, so they should move. Please don't complain that sons and daughters of politicians and corporate executives are not fighting and dying for America in foreign lands. Corporations are doing their bit by "donating" the missiles, the planes, the bombs, the ammunition, the foodstuffs, the footwear, and the body bags. Does it cost a few million dollars, every hour, every day, to pursue our various wars? No way, sir and madam. It's all donated, with Blinky, Cheney Dick, and all their corporate buddies writing personal checks to cover the whole tab.

So, you see, it borders on calumny to suggest that the accidental and temporary White House resident knows anything about rewarding corporations and rich friends with tax cuts, or that he had any idea that Enron had contributed hundreds of thousands of dollars to his various campaigns. So, knock it off.

As a matter of fact, it's absurd to suggest that Blinky knows anything about anything at all, so knock it off.

Windfalls
for the
Rich

Where is this "compassionate conservatism"?

WHILE SCANDALS BREAK as regularly as waves on the beach, and taxpayers are milked of trillions of dollars, given as tax breaks to the wealthy, so-called "homeless shelters" are loaded beyond capacity beyond anything seen in years.

Now, let me interject that the term "homeless shelter" is a misnomer, even though educated people intone it sonorously on television and radio. It's *people* who are homeless: thinking, feeling, caring, despairing people; fearful, crying, ailing children, cringing, sick addicts, tormented with mental problems. "Shelters" are structures rooted in one spot, but to refer to them as "homeless" serves to diminish the plight of those who are. The term reminds me of "near miss," which is an almost-hit, but a 100 percent miss in the final tally.

This winter, over 38,000 people in New York alone, almost half of them children under 18, were in shelters for the homeless. Now, let's just get past the morality lecture on why these mothers should keep their nether limbs shut and discuss the facts. Frightened and dislocated children are dragged from office to office, and thence to maddeningly noisy, dangerous and overcrowded warehouses (called "residences").

So, where, oh where, is this much-vaunted "compassionate conservatism" here? Two tokens of it, offered by Blinky and his brother, might be the electric chair and the gas chamber, but those might prove too expensive with the current severe energy crisis. And, Great Kills, the huge rubbish landfill in Staten Island, New York, is closed now, so we can't dump the poor there, and if we feed them to the cattle, there's a distinct chance that innocent bovines will contract Mad People Disease (the mad ones are those who inexplicably voted for Bush).

My compassion for these unfortunate folks is not hard to explain. When the McCourt family returned to Ireland in the early '30s (remember: Frank and I were born in the U.S.), we found no welcome at the paternal grand-parents' home outside of Belfast, so we somehow piled the family of six onto a train, which took us only as far as Dublin, for we had no money to make it to Limerick, a further 120 miles away.

Around Dublin we trudged, seeking food and shelter on that chilling and rainy night, we children constantly looking at the parental face in search of reassurance that everything was going to be all right. From our toddlers' perspective, all we saw was lengthening shadows and deep furrows on their brows, and no sign of light, save the occasional glisten of a tear. In response to our pleas, all we got from the Dubliners was: "Can't help you," and condemnation for having so many children and dragging them around the city.

No evidence was there of "Irish hospitality," nor any generosity at all, so we ended up bunking in the little jail in a local police station, being fed sandwiches by some kind policemen.

The next day, again helped by the police, we boarded the train to Limerick, but a few years later, after my father left us, we were evicted from our slum dwelling, because we couldn't afford the six-shilling ($1-a-week) rent.

We do not live in Depression-era Ireland now. Money that is wasted hiring housekeepers and drivers for admirals and generals could be used to build houses and apartments for people on the streets. Isn't the single purpose of government to provide for the welfare of its citizens? All of them?

Instead, we now give "constitutional rights" to corporations, which are profit-making entities, not people. In reality, actual people have fewer rights than big corporations, which are allowed to deduct, for tax purposes, equipment purchases and depreciation of desks, airplanes, yachts, automobiles, electronic stuff, and even buildings.

Since I work for myself, I would like to be able to deduct myself and the depreciation of my eyes, ears, teeth, knees, lungs, and every other organ, not to mention my memory, which goes on strike at the slightest provocation. But will the IRS let me do that? Not on your Nellie! Will the corporation get its deduction for the country club and the golf outing? Of course, darling!

Of course, Blinky and the Dick are believers in Jesus, who said that the poor will always be with us, so what's the point of doing anything for them? Let them eat caviar and live in a McMansion.

The
Symptom:
Sickentired;
the
Disease:
Conservatism

"These People,"
"I pay my taxes," and
other dark Leitmotifs

REPUBLICANS ARE NOTED for being very moral and also very compassionate. Not everyone understands the tremendous burden of having the lion's share of the nation's wealth whilst the goddam poor clamor for services they ill deserve: medical care, schools for their children, decent housing, equitable legal treatment, clean air, water, parks for recreation. Worst of all, they expect some of this be paid for by those with the most money.

And those same, ungrateful bastards never say a word of

thank you, and when we send their children to die in Iraq, Afghanistan, Kosovo, and Somalia, they bitch constantly.

Footwear, both leather and canvas, presents a double dilemma to Republicans. They enrich themselves from sneaker factories manned by underage Asians, yet they prattle on about "pulling themselves up by their own bootstraps." How can we unravel this paradox? Well, if you have the monopoly on the boots, all you need do is marry into the family supplying the straps, and you're on the stairway to the stars. We now know, after reading *American Dynasty*, by Kevin Phillips, that the Bush family is on top through sheer entitlement.

So, just as obesity is a genetic disease, the Bush presidential dynasty is an irremediable affliction we must endure as stoically as the plagues of the Middle Ages. Working people now submit to the inevitability of this blight. Conservatives, especially in right-wing rags such as the *New York Post* (thank you, Rupert Murdoch), always bemoan that they are "sickentired" of this or that—not just "sick," never just "tired," not even "illenfatigued," but simply that they are "sickentired." Not only do they work hard, but they inform us that "I pay my taxes." Not, mind you, government taxes, but "my taxes."

Further, these self-styled American conservatives single out a particular class of folks they refer to as "these people." "These people" usually include the poor, often of a color not white, who have endured racism, lynchings, discrimination, and all other forms of bigotry. Often, they have children out of wedlock. For these reasons, "these people" are branded as "un-American," and thus qualify for deportation or indeterminate jail terms, where they will be out of sight and out of mind.

The father of Arnold Gropenführer, the current governor of California, and the layer-on of hands on unwilling women, had a father who was an ardent admirer of Adolf Hitler. Though I, too, had a less-than-admirable father, and I was occasionally less than kind to women, I drew the line at admiring Adolf, or Benito, or Ashcroft, or Blinky bin Bush, so I can claim my distance from Blinky and the Republican Texiban.

Not so for that fine, upstanding, flag-waving American, Rush Limbaugh, who, though admittedly guilty of drug abuse, that most unforgivable of crimes in America, is still *sickentired* of liberals and their liberal press (owned, curiously, by Murdoch, Disney, G.E. Westinghouse, and Clear Channel Communications), trying to curtail our rights to own guns, charge as much as we like for prescription drugs, and invade any nation which happens to interfere with "American interests."

My People-Pleasing Days

At least now they're over

Just in case you didn't know it, I am a very clever fellow. Cleverness is best accompanied by cunning, though it seems one can be both cunning and dimwitted, as in the case of Blinky bin Bush and his Corporate Tabernacle Choir. My cleverness, though, emerged from the need to survive a physically and emotionally miserable childhood, so I learned to get what I needed by letting people think that it was their idea, instead of me soliciting whatever it was.

Indeed, I was a charming little fellow, so Aryan-looking that I could have been a poster child for the Hitler Youth, had I been born in Nazi Germany. But I wasn't, so slumhood in Ireland was my lot. A song called "Come Back, Paddy Reilly," evokes those days:

> "My mother once told me that when I was born,
> The day that I first saw the light
> I looked down the street on that very first morn
> And gave a great crow of delight
> Now most newborn babies appear in a huff
> And start with a sorrowful squall
> But I knew I was born in Ballyjamesduff
> And that's why I smiled on them all."

As a kid, I took quickly to the people-pleasing ruse. So, at church, I looked angelic whilst planning to rob the collection plate (though I never did). At school, I appeared respectful (though stupid), whilst planning to murder the masters, who whacked us with sticks and thumped us with their fists, but, outside of a bit of vandalism, I didn't damage anyone or anything. In the end, I wasn't helped at all by my reptilian sense of self-esteem, since there's nothing more irritating than a needy, snivelling victim of life, however charming.

I've found it takes some maturity to assert yourself as a full-fledged citizen of planet earth. Some deluded souls think we are blessed by God or Allah in having Blinky or bin Laden as our leaders in the Good Fight. Earlier on, others were enamored of A. Hitler and B. Mussolini; still others worshipped J. Stalin or Attila the Hun, or Ilsa Koch, the Bitch of Buchenwald, or Margaret Thatcher, or Joseph McCarthy, and so on. But developing the fiber to make your own moral choices and ethical opinions can take some time, if it happens at all.

Thus, if some polls are correct, not too many people think it's savage to bomb a defenseless people, or to let thousands of children (say, in Iraq) starve to death. The rest apparently go about, with flags aflutter, asking God to bless America and its bombs, rockets, and planes that reduce the bodies of humans to slivers of bone and shreds of skin, as the Deity sits in His love seat, egging us all on.

So, here I am, dry-cleaned spiritually (I hope) and praying that Blinky Bush will have the moral strength to give back the Enron money and return the millions stolen from the taxpayers of Texas. May they realize that only people with intelligence and integrity should occupy the White House.

I have written to Blinky and asked him to find it in his Christian heart to forgive the terrorist who launched the pretzel attack on him last year (he nearly choked to death, as you'll recall). He may be dissuaded from bombing the pretzel factories.

Confessions
of a
Curmudgeon

I'M AT AN AGE when I find I'm what people label a "curmudgeon." Like a lot of the liberal-minded, I'm a seething mass of prejudices, judgments, critical opinions, intolerances, and dislikes. Am I bigoted? No, but I probably sail close to the wind on that one sometimes.

If I were in the position to employ someone, I'd probably ascertain first if he or she was a smoker. If a smoker, then I'd put 'em in the half-wit column and suggest a rehabilitation clinic 'til a cure was in hand.

Conservatives are Nazis waiting to happen, while "compassionate conservatives" are not alone Nazis waiting in the wings, but lying swine as well (apologies here to my innocent friends in the pig family).

Others I'd ostracize:

- People who bellow into cell phones in public, as if I have an intense interest in their grandchild's diapering; if they're driving, cell phone use might have almost cost me my life for the umpteenth time.

○ Politicians who claim to be Democrats and who vote Republican.

○ Nitwits who try to carry on a conversation whilst headphones blast noise into their ear canals.

○ Drivers in boom cars loud enough to activate other cars' alarms;

○ Any SUV driver.

○ Any Humvee driver.

○ People constantly proclaiming their "Americanism."

○ People who hit children.

○ Any McDonald's.

○ Any Burger King.

○ Any Banana Republic.

○ Any cola.

○ People who say, "I'm the kind that speaks my mind," or rubbish like that.

○ Conniving Irish, Italians, blacks, Jews, and working class, who betray their heritage by becoming Republicans.

○ Those who deride Big Government but accept unemployment insurance, Medicare, medicaid, welfare, and Social Security, forgetting that F.D.R., L.B.J.,

and others had to fight for these programs against
Republicans, who denounced them as "communism."

- People who wouldn't know rat piss from Ripple talking about wine.

- Blinky bin Bush's current face. I doubt the Wanker
  is two-faced, as he could hardly have chosen the disgusting one he wears nowadays.

- Rabid patriots, who talk from the safety of an arm-
  chair about what should be done to Osama, Iraqi
  insurgents, and other terrorists.

- People who are late for the theater.

- News readers who are called "anchors."

- People who chew gum and spit it out anywhere they
  please.

- People who use the word "fight" in their speeches.
  Whom will they fight?

- And let's not forget golf, golfing, and golfers, impotent people compensating for the lack of a life with all
  the Freudian symbols, like clubs, poles, balls, and
  holes. The environment is devastated by the overuse
  of pesticides and water in nurturing the golf courses,
  and the golfing fools even avoid a bit of exercise by
  using golf carts.

- Then, there's Wanker Bush, who still refuses to give
  a decent accounting to the 9/11 investigators, having

withheld from them hundreds of documents to protect his corrupt Saudi pals. Bush hopes to remain in the office he stole, while Halliburton and the Carlyle Group of bin Bushes, bin Cheneys, bin Ladens, and all the other bins, will continue swimming in money and destroying the world.

The fumigators are standing by, ready, after the end of Blinky bin Bush's reign of error, to clean the scum and filth out of the White House after January 20, 2005.

The
Year
the
Wanker
Won
the
Penance

A Bush-basher acknowledges the error of his cruel ways

ONE PERSON WAS ASKING me where I've been these last few weeks, and several thousand have said, "Good riddance, who gives a shite?" I went into seclusion to rethink all my positions on various issues, and not alone have I been wrong, oh so wrong on so many things. I have been cruel to those who disagreed with me. And I cannot comprehend how people can question the workings of our democratic system, or the word and honor of our great president, George Wanker Bush.

For weeks now I've sat swathed in sackcloth, with my household staff kept busy pouring ashes over my cranium. Being too overcome with remorse and too tired to do it myself, I had my valet beat my breast whilst a chorus of personal assistants, housemaids, and outside staff chanted, "Mea culpa, mea maxima culpa!" For penance, I reduced my intake of filet mignon to once a day, and caviar to every other day, and instead of being carried to my Rolls Royce, I actually walked to it.

Due to my personal transformation, I am now a True Believer, and have arranged for a hundred lambs to be slaughtered so that I can bathe in their blood. I had three-quarters of my brain removed, and am now a full-fledged conservative, 100 percent compassionate, so I now approve of killing people to put them out of their misery.

Now that I am "saved" and bathed in the light, the truth is finally dawning on me. How dare those rotten Democrats accuse our dear George Wanker, his bro, Jeb Wanker, and their ally, Katherine Wankee of stealing the presidency? Nothing but sore losers. They can't take a joke.

This same crowd of traitors is urging us to read the lies of Paul O'Neill and Richard Clarke, with their leaking of confidential material. Don't they know that if we Americans learn the truth about our dear Wanker, he might lose the election to John Kerry? Just because Kerry got wounded and wears a chestful of medals doesn't mean he's a hero.

George, on the other hand, is modest about his heroism during his initiation into the Skull and Bones society at Yale. The full details of this ritual cannot be printed, since they are too graphic for public consumption, but I can reveal that one requirement was for W to do kaka in the president's garden and not get caught. How does Kerry's heroism compare with this? Pshaw! It's now clear to me that Wanker's money and family name are burdens, not joys.

When Daddy told jolly stories about when he was boss of the Central Intelligence Agency, and the fun they had poisoning, stabbing, and otherwise eliminating thousands of perceived enemies, the young Wanker could only feel inadequate because of the tiny number of people he executed in Texas— a mere 131. Of course, he yearned to become President so that he could be a big man and kill thousands (in the name of God).

I know our beloved Wanker is dedicated to preventing those homos from getting wed and putting their weewees in each other's bottoms, when everyone in Texas knows the proper place for a weewee is in a cow's bottom (provided no co-ed is available).

How despicable are those who want to remove "under God" from the pledge of allegiance to the flag! Every soldier who has the privilege of wearing the uniform should be recorded saying the pledge, and this recording should be placed in his coffin so his relatives can hear his voice as it emanates from under the flag. Then they can praise God and bless George W. Bush for allowing their child to be killed in defense of America. Don't expect George W to be at the ceremony, though, since he has to attend hundreds of fund-raisers, rodeos, and concerts, so he doesn't have time to go to the funerals of the more than 800 young Americans killed in Iraq. Bush also prevents the press from attending the funerals, because he knows how sad these occasions can be.

About the Turkey Who Flew to Iraq

A holiday fable about Bush's war and Bush's secret trip

LAST THANKSGIVING, whilst we were wolfing down dead birds, sweet potatoes, and pumpkin pies, our joy and gratitude coincided with one of the biggest operations in the history of warfare. Even D-Day plans were dwarfed by its magnitude. Here was the deal.

A few Thanksgivings ago, the squatter in the White House conducted a ceremony of public compassion wherein he pardoned a turkey. In case you're unaware, compassionate conservatism allows for pardoning turkeys, perjurers, lying former presidents, and marines who swear falsely, but never people suffering from learning difficulties or mental health problems.

So, then, our turkey: as you know, the nation of Turkey wouldn't allow the U.S. Armed Forces on its soil to launch an attack on Iraq, although they did send troops to kill potential terrorists—Iraqi school kids. So, whether it's "turkey" the bird, or "Turkey," the country, trouble looms large.

Anyway, back on last November 27, we found our near-future-former faux President on his pitiful little 1,600-acre ranch, surrounded by a fluttering coterie of other liars and hypocrites, about to pardon a large, feathered being—a turkey. And as said pardon was about to be pronounced, what did this turkey do? He decided to impersonate a silly goose by giving Blinky a shock and shoving his beak under Blinky's coat, the area obscuring his fly. What happened then is classified "top secret," but, judging from Blinky's expression, 'twas not unwelcome. Indeed, it must have conjured memories of old Skull and Bones initiations at Yale. Nonetheless, 'twas just a hypocritical turkey expressing thanks at Thanksgiving, promising never to say a word to other turkeys, who would probably have done things unprintable here if their lives might be spared.

But—what has happened to that turkey since then? He went back to the farm, where he was recruited by a terrorist group for underfeather work. They converted him from a laid-again Christian egg to a paradise-bound fundamentalist egg. Since he had known the faux-president and the bumblings of his administrations intimately, the fundamentalists were certain he was no cuckoo.

So, joining a flock of geese, our turkey fled the coop and made for Iraq, where he began his training as an underfeather agent.

You can only imagine the rage of Blinky bin Bush, when Rummy and St. Faschroft informed him of the turkey's defection. Blinky railed about being betrayed by a fowl who had been so close to him, both physically and spiritually, with their mutual interest in laying turkey eggs (or anything else), but *now* it had defected to our enemy, who never liked turkeys or even the bushes they hide under.

Blinky had the army's camouflage experts disguise Air Force One as a turkey, and Air Force Two as a flying snake, and the escort fleet as cuckoos, and off they went to Baghdad on Thanksgiving morn to trap that traitorous turkey, who knew too much. When the cuckoo-in-chief landed in Iraq, there were thousands of Iraqis disguised as turkeys, but Blinky wasn't fooled. There was only one big bird with that beak he knew so well. And so began a massive search for the treacherous turkey. Forget Osama bin Laden, forget the insurgents, forget weapons of mass destruction, forget the Iraqi kids getting killed (only two that day, it turned out)! Get that turkey and dispatch him with all conservative compassion! The mission was tough, but they finally caught that turkey nuzzling a fallen statue of Saddam Hussein.

So, reversing his presidential pardon, Blinky had the feathered enemy slain, and gathered 130,000 American troops in the main square of Baghdad, where the traitorous bird produced endless slices and drumsticks for the cheering personnel, happy that, though they were being killed and wounded, a vicious enemy had been taken down and eaten.

Then, Blinky and his fellow patriots fled Iraq oh-so-quickly, and 'twas back to the ranch and the hugs of Big Blinky, who rejoiced at not having to bury his son, like so many other fathers around the country.

Born in Brooklyn, New York, **Malachy McCourt** was raised from the age of three in Limerick, Ireland, where a highly undistinguished academic career (plus the need to eat) led him to leave school at age thirteen to begin work as a laborer.

At the age of twenty, he returned to the land of his birth, where he again took up the manual trades, such as longshoreman, truck loader, and dishwasher, until he became an actor. That career took him to Broadway, off-Broadway, regional theater, movies, as well as numerous soap operas and cable television.

In the early seventies, a lively and controversial time of his life, he was one of the first radio talk show hosts on WMCA in New York City, where he was also a frequent guest on *The Tonight Show*, and the Merv Griffin and Tom Snyder shows. He has been credited with founding the first singles bar in America, Malachy's of Third Avenue.

As a writer, Malachy coauthored and costarred with his brother Frank in the play, *A Couple of Blaguards*, and wrote a best-selling memoir, *A Monk Swimming* (Hyperion Press). His most recent memoir, *Singing My Him Song*, was published by HarperCollins and his book-length histories of the song "Danny Boy" and "The Claddagh Ring" were published by Running Press.

His latest book is *Harold Be Thy Name* (Carhil Ventures), and soon to be published is *I Never Drink When I'm Sober* (HarperCollins). His column, "Sez I to Myself," appears weekly in *The Manhattan Spirit*, *The Westsider*, and *Our Town*, New York City newspapers.

Malachy has been happily married to Diana for almost four decades, has five children, and is grandfather to four. He owes a great deal to his friend Bill W.